誠 MAKOTO

e-zine for learners of Japanese

ご 購入
ありがとう
ございます。

（こうにゅう）

Thank you so much
for your purchase!

I know what you are thinking. "*Kicchomu again?!*" Well, yes, but don't worry. We are running out of Kicchomu stories.

I'm just kidding. I know you are really thinking: "*Yeah! Kicchomu again!*" But it is true we are running out of stories about him. Enjoy this issue's story while we are still on our Kicchomu kick.

Last month, we celebrated our four year and 50th issue anniversary. Want to keep getting Makoto each month for as long as we continue to publish? (We have absolutely no plans to stop—this is too much fun) Become a Makoto+ lifetime member now:

https://makotoplus.com/lifetime-makoto/

Not only will you download the latest issue each month for as long as there is Makoto, but you'll also get full access to the website forever. Lifetime is the same as Shogun, but without the pesky monthly bills.

Click the above link to learn more.

Clay & Yumi

P.S. The ninja on the cover says, 元気かい *genki kai,* which means, "Are you doing all right?"

In this Issue:

LAUGHS, JOKES, RIDDLES, AND PUNS

コンビニで

おじいさん: 肉（にく）まんください。

店員（てんいん）: おいくつですか？（おじいさんは、年齢（ねんれい）を聞（き）かれていると思（おも）ったが、店員（てんいん）は肉（にく）まんの数（かず）を聞（き）いている）

おじいさん: いくつに見（み）えますか？

店員（てんいん）: えっと、いくつでしょうか？

おじいさん: もう８０（はちじゅう）ですよ。

店員（てんいん）: はい、肉（にく）まん８０個（はちじゅっこ）、8000円（はっせんえん）になります。

おじいさん: いや、そうじゃなくて。

店員（てんいん）: 8000円（はっせんえん）です。

おじいさん: ・・・

At a Convenience Store

Old man: Steamed meat bun, please.

Clerk: *Oikutsu desu ka* (How many? / How old are you?) (The old man thought he was being asked his age, but the clerk was asking for the quantity of the meat buns.)

Continued

Old man: How old do I look?

Clerk: Uhh... *ikutsu deshou ka* (How many? / How old are you?)?

Old man: I'm already 80.

Clerk: OK, 80 steamed meat buns, that will be 8,000 yen.

Old man: No, that's not what I meant.

Clerk: It's 8,000 yen.

Old man: ...

<u>Vocabulary:</u>

ジョーク *jo-ku*—a joke

コンビニ *konbini*—convenience store

で *de*—at; in [indicates the location of action]

おじいさん *ojiisan*—old man; male senior-citizen; grandfather

肉まんください *nikuman kudasai*—steamed meat bun, please [**肉まん** (steamed meat bun) + **くだ さい** (please (give me))]

店員 *tenin*—employee (of a store); shop assistant; clerk; salesperson

おいくつ *oikutsu*—how many; how old [**お** (honorific/polite/humble prefix) + **いくつ** (how many; how old)]

です *desu*—be; is

か *ka*—(question marker)

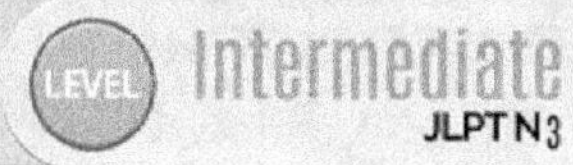

Vocabulary Continued

おじいさんは *ojiisan wa*—the old man [**おじいさん** (old man) + **は** (indicates the sentence topic)]

年齢を聞かれてる *nenrei o kikarete ru*—is being asked (his) age [**年齢**(ねんれい) (age; years) + **を** (indicates the direct object of action) + **聞(き)かれてる** (てる-form of **聞(き)かれる** (plain passive positive form of **聞(き)く** (to ask; to enquire; to query)); ~**てる** is casual form of ~**ている** which is used to describe an ongoing action; how to form: Verb **て**-form + **る**)]

と思った *to omotta*—thought [**と** (used for quoting (thoughts, speech, etc.)) + **思(おも)った** (thought; plain past form of **思(おも)う** (to think; to consider; to believe))]

が *ga*—but; however

店員は *tenin wa*—the clerk [**店員**(てんいん) (employee (of a store); clerk) + **は** (indicates the sentence topic)]

肉まんの数 *nikuman no kazu*—quantity of the meat buns [**肉まん**(にく) (steamed meat bun) + **の** (of; modifier) + **数** (quantity; number of)]

を *o*—(indicates the direct object of action)

聞いている *kiite iru*—is/are asking; ask [**ている**-form of **聞(き)く** (to ask) which is used to describe an ongoing action; how to form: Verb **て**-form + **いる**]

いくつに見えますか *ikutsu ni miemasu ka*—How old do (I) look? [**いくつ** (how old; how many) + **に見(み)えます** (to look; to appear) + **か** (question marker)]

えっと *etto*—errr ...; uhh ...

いくつでしょうか *ikutsu deshou ka*—how many?; how old are you? [**いくつ** (how old; how many)

Vocabulary Continued

+ **でしょうか** (polite question marker)]

もう80 *mou hachi juu*—already 80 [**もう** (already; by now)]

ですよ *desu yo*—(sentence ender showing assertion or confidence; is used in spoken Japanese and informal situations)

はい *hai*—yes; I see; OK; okay

80個 *hachi jukko*—80 (buns); 80 pcs [個 is a counter for articles]

8000円 *hassen en*—8000 yen [円 (Japanese monetary unit)]

になります *ni narimasu*—come to; turn out to; become [**に** (expresses the result of change) **＋ なります** (**ます**/polite form of **なる** (to become; to turn))]

いや *iya*—no!

そうじゃなくて *sou ja nakute*—that's not what (I) meant

8000円です *hassen en desu*—it's 8000 yen [円 (yen; Japanese monetary unit) + **です** (be; is)]

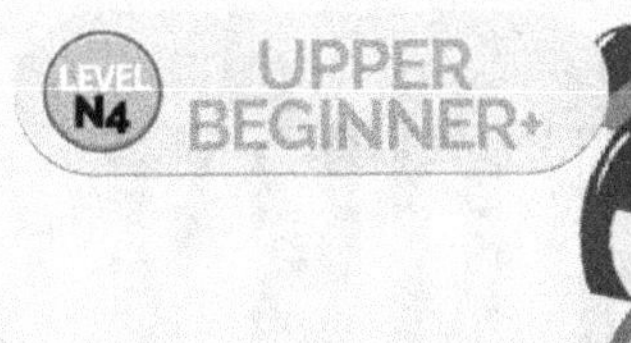

VOCABULARY

Learn Useful Words, Phrases, and Sayings

けんえん　なか
犬猿の仲

ken'en no naka

on bad terms; hate each other's guts; fight like cats and dogs

ⓘ When you just can't get along with someone, your relationship is like that of a dog (*ken*) and monkey (*en*).

> "The relationship between dogs and monkeys." This saying came about because it is said in Japan that dogs and monkeys do not naturally get along.

EXAMPLE SENTENCE:

ふたり　　あ
あの二人は、会ったらすぐにけんかをはじめてしまう。
けんえん　なか
犬猿の仲だ。

ano futari wa, attara sugu ni kenka o hajimete shimau.

kenen no naka da.

Those two start bickering as soon as they meet. Just like cats and dogs.

VOCABULARY:

あの二人 *ano futari*—those two (people)

会ったら *attara*—if (they) meet; upon meeting; when seeing (each other) [会
(verb stem of 会う (to meet)) + たら (upon~; when~; if~); たら **Construction**:
conjugate the preceding verb into the past form and add ら：会う→会った→

Vocabulary Continued

会ったら]

すぐに *sugu ni*—soon; right away

けんか *kenka*—fight; bickering

を *o*—(a particle which indicates the direct object of action)

はじめて *hajimete*— begins [*te*-form of はじめる (to begin; to start)]

しまう *shimau*—unfortunately (start fighting) [(~て)しまう indicates the situation to be unfavorable]

の *no*—[modifying particle that connects the modifying word and the word being modified]

仲 *naka*—relation; relationship

犬猿の仲 *kenen no naka*—fight like cats and dogs [Literally, "relationship of dog and monkey"; 犬 (dog) + 猿 (monkey) + ~の仲 (relationship of ~); example: 仲のよい兄弟 (brothers who are on good terms)]

だ *da*—plain form of です copula (be; is)

Yamanashi 山梨

Japanese: 山梨県 *yamanashi ken*

Capital: 甲府 Kōfu

Population: 817,192 (January 1, 2019)

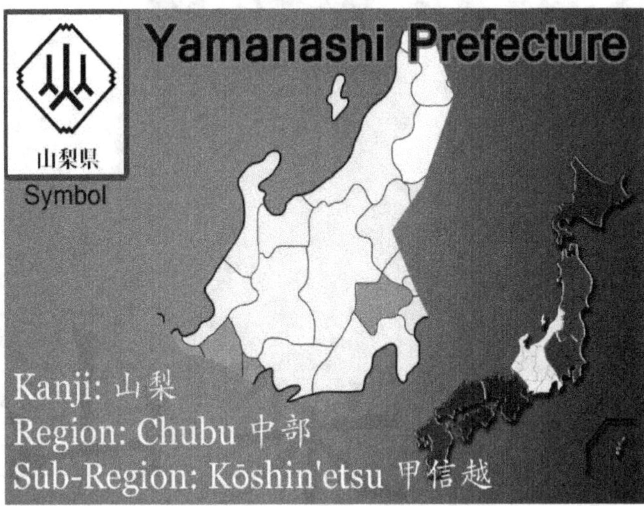

DID YOU KNOW?

The inland prefecture Yamanashi means "mountain pear" and Mt. Fuji borders Yamanashi and Shizuoka prefectures.

PLACES TO SEE:

- **Mt. Fuji**—the northern half is in Yamanashi prefecture.

- **The Fuji Five Lakes Region**—located at the foot of Mt. Fuji, this is a great place for hiking, camping, and fishing, as well as viewing Mt. Fuji.

- **Fuji-Q Highland**—a major amusement park near Mt. Fuji. It is famous for its roller coasters, anime-themed rides, and Thomas Land, a children's area with a Thomas the Tank Engine theme.

- **Shosenkyo Gorge**—a beautiful gorge found in the Chichibu Tama Kai National Park. It is particularly spectacular during the autumn when the leaves change color.

FAMOUS FOR:

- **Robotics industry.**

- **Major fruit producer** in Japan (grapes, peaches, plums).

- About 40% of the **mineral water** bottled in Japan comes from Yamanashi, taken from the Southern Alps and Mt. Fuji.

- **Koshu Wine**—the more than 80 wineries in Katsunuma produce about **40% of Japan's domestic wine**.

- **Takeda Shingen**—the famous feudal warlord was born in the area now called Yamanashi.

「セレブ」

"Serebu"

Scan for Recording

日本語の「セレブ」という言葉は、英語の「セレブリティー」から来ています。英語のセレブリティーは、とても人気がある有名人とか、誰もが知っている俳優さんなどをさす言葉ですが、日本では「セレブ」と短く略して使われるようになりました。最近は「お金持ち」という意味でも使われるようになりました。有名でなくても、高級な服装をしていたり、豪華で大きな家に住んでいる人のことを「セレブ」と呼ぶようになったのです。

The Japanese word "*serebu*" comes from the English word "celebrity". The English word "celebrity" refers to a very popular celebrity or an actor whom everyone knows, but in Japan it is shortened to "*serebu*" and used as an abbreviation. Recently, it has come to be used to also mean "rich". Even if they are not famous, but wear expensive clothes

Continued

or live in luxurious and large houses, they have come to be called "*serebu*."

Vocabulary

語源 etymology; origin of a word

「セレブ」 "serebu" [「」 (quotation marks; " ") + セレブ (serebu)]

日本語の 「セレブ」 the Japanese "serebu" [日本語 (Japanese (language)) + の (of; 's; modifier) + 「セレブ」 ("serebu")]

という named; called; such a/an [is used to define, describe, and generally just talk about the thing itself]

言葉 word; phrase; term

は (indicates the sentence topic)

英語の 「セレブリティー」 the English "celebrity" [英語 (English (language)) + の (of; modifier) + 「セレブリティー」 ("celebrity")]

から from

来ています come; is/are coming; has come [ています-form of 来る (to come) which is used to describe a continuous action; how to form: Verb て-form + います]

英語のセレブリティーは the English celebrity [英語 (English) + の (modifier) + セレブリティー (celebrity) + は (indicates the sentence topic)]

とても very; exceedingly

人気がある popular; star; be liked by everybody

有名人 celebrity; famous person; public figure [有名 (famous) + 人 (person; someone; somebody)]

とか and/or [connecting particle which is used to list multiple things of the same kind, and imply there are other items that could be included in the list]

誰も everyone; anyone [When used with a negative verb, this can mean "no one."]

Vocabulary Continued

が (identifies who performs the action; emphasizes the preceding word)

知っている know; knowing [ている-form of 知る (to know; to be familiar with) which is used to describe some continuous action or events; how to use: Verb て-form + いる]

俳優さん actor; actress; player; performer [俳優 (actor; actress; player; performer) + さん (politeness marker; is used after a noun or sometimes な-adjective)]

など et cetera; etc.; and the like; and so forth

を (indicates the direct object of action)

さす言葉 a word that refers to [さす (refer; identify; indicate; point out) + 言葉 (word; term; phrase)]

です be; is

が but

日本では in Japan [日本 (Japan) + で (at; in; indicates the location of action) + は (indicates the sentence topic)]

「セレブ」と "serebu" [「セレブ」 ("serebu") + と (quotation marker)]

短く short [continuative form of 短い (short; brief) which is used to connect to the next verb]

略して shortened to ("serebu") and [て-form of 略する (cut; abbreviate; shorten; reduce) which is used to connect to the next phrase, creating the meaning of "and"]

使われる is/are used [plain passive positive form of 使う (to use (a tool, method, etc.))]

ようになりました came to be that; has/have become; became [polite past form of ようになる (to become; to come to be that; to turn into ~; to reach the point that); how to form: Verb (dictionary/ない form) + ようになりました]

最近は recently [最近 (recently; lately; these days; nowadays; right now) + は (adds emphasis)]

「お金持ち」という意味 mean/means "rich" [「お金持ち」 ("rich; rich person") + という (named; called; such; is used to define, describe, and generally just talk about the thing itself) +

Vocabulary Continued

意味 (meaning; significance; sense)]

でも also; as well

使われるようになりました (it) has come to be used [使われる (is/are used) + ようになりました (has/have come)]

有名でなくても even if not famous [有名 (famous) + でなくて (casual form of ではなくて (it is not that; describes a negation)) + も (even; even if; even though ~)]

高級な luxury; high-grade; expensive; fancy

服装をしていたり wear expensive (clothes) or [from 服装をする (wear; dress); ~たり means "and/or" which is used to list representative activities in which there may be additional activities that are not mentioned; how to form: Verb (た form) + り]

豪華で luxurious and [豪華 (luxurious; magnificent; splendid; fancy; lavish) + で (て-form of です which is used to connect to the next phrase, creating the meaning of "and")]

大きな big; large; great

家に住んでいる live in (luxurious) house [家 (house; residence; dwelling) + に (in; expresses the location of existence) + 住んでいる (ている-form of 住む (to live (of humans); to reside; to inhabit; to dwell) which is used to describe the actual state or condition of the subject)]

人のこと all the things about the person [人 (person; someone; somebody) + のこと (all the things about; it has a "focusing" feature and lets you know that the subject has a certain quality; how to form: Noun + のこと)]

を (indicates the direct object of action)

「セレブ」と呼ぶようになった came to be called "serebu" [「セレブ」 ("serebu") + と (quotation marker) + 呼ぶ (to call out (to); to call) + ようになった (came to be that)]

のです it is that …; the fact is that …; the explanation is that; the reason is that … [explanatory ender]

ANIME / MANGA PHRASE

Surprise your Japanese friends with these phrases

Please see the sound files for the pronunciation

<ruby>俺<rt>おれ</rt></ruby>は<ruby>人間<rt>にんげん</rt></ruby>をやめるぞ。

「俺は人間をやめるぞ。ジョジョ ～!!」

ディオ・ブランドのセリフ

「ジョジョの<ruby>奇妙<rt>きみょう</rt></ruby>な<ruby>冒険<rt>ぼうけん</rt></ruby>」より

Scan for Recording

「ore wa ningen o yameru zo. jojo~!!」

dio burando no serifu

「jojo no kimyouna bouken」 yori

"I reject my humanity. Jojo!!"
Line from Dio Brando
From "JoJo's Bizarre Adventure"

VOCABULARY

「」 —(quotation marks; " ")

俺 *ore*—I; me [male term or language, rough or arrogant]

は *wa*—(indicates the sentence topic)

人間 *ningen*—human being; human; person; man; mankind; humankind

ANIME / MANGA PHRASE

Surprise your Japanese friends with these phrases

Continued

を *o*—(indicates the direct object of action)

やめる *yameru*—to quit; to give up; to abandon; to abolish

ぞ *zo*—(sentence ender that adds force spoken by males)

ジョジョ〜 *jojo~* —Jojo

ディオ・ブランドのセリフ *dio.burando no serifu*—Line from Dio Brando [ディオ・ブランド (Dio Brando) + の (of; from; modifier) + セリフ (one's lines; speech; words)]

「ジョジョの奇妙な冒険」 *「jojo no kimyouna bouken」* —"JoJo's Bizarre Adventure" [「」 (quotation marks; " ") + ジョジョ (Jojo) + の (of; 's; modifier) + 奇妙な きみょう (bizarre; fantastic; peculiar) + 冒険 ぼうけん (adventure; venture)]

「ジョジョの奇妙な冒険」より *「jojo no kimyouna bouken」 yori*—from "JoJo's Bizarre Adventure" [「ジョジョの奇妙な冒険」 きみょう ぼうけん ("JoJo's Bizarre Adventure") + より (from)]

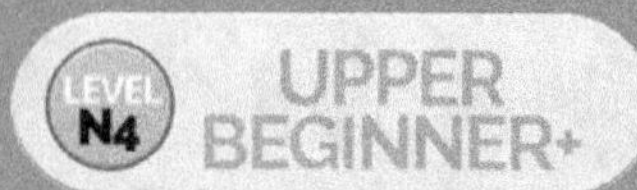

Kobayashi Issa 小林一茶
こばやしいっさ

大江戸や　犬もありつく　初鰹
（おおえど）　（いぬ）　（はつがつお）

oo edo ya / inu mo aritsuku / hatsugatsuo

Big city of Edo | dogs also get | the season's first bonito

Haiku Audio

Explanation:

季語: 初鰹
（きご）（はつがつお）

大きな江戸の町で、初鰹が売られ始めた。犬も
（おお）（えど）（まち）（はつがつお）（う）（はじ）（いぬ）

喜んで食べている。
（よろこ）（た）

Explanation

Season term: The first bonito of the season (*Hatsugatsuo*)

In the big city of Edo, the first bonito of the season has begun to be sold. Even the dogs are happy to eat it.

Vocabulary

大江戸 big city of Edo [大 (large; big; great; huge; vast) + 江戸 (Edo
（おお）　　　　　　　　　　　　　　　　　　　　　　　（えど）

Continued

(shogunate capital, now Tokyo))]

や (emphasizes the preceding word) [it's a *kireji* (cutting word) which indicates a pause, both rhythmically and grammatically, and may add an emotional flavor to the word/phrase preceding it]

犬 dog

も too; also; even

ありつく get; obtain; acquire

初鰹 the first bonito of the season [初 (first; new) + 鰹 (か changes to a が; skipjack tuna (Katsuwonus pelamis); oceanic bonito; victorfish)]

季語 seasonal word (in haiku)

大きな big; large; great

江戸の町 city of Edo [江戸 (Edo (shogunate capital, now Tokyo)) + の (of; modifier) + 町 (city; town)]

で in; at [indicates the location of action]

が (emphasizes the preceding word 初鰹 (the first bonito of the season))

売られ始めた has begun to be sold [売られ is the ます-stem form of 売られます (polite passive positive form of 売る (to sell) which is used to connect to the next verb 始めた (begun; plain past form of 始める (to start; to begin)))]

Vocabulary Continued

犬も even dogs [犬 (いぬ) (dogs) + も (even)]

喜んで with pleasure; happily; gladly [て-form (adverbial form) of 喜 (よろこ) ぶ (to be glad; to be de-

lighted) which is used to modify the next verb 食 (た) べている (eat; eating)]

食べている eat; eating [ている-form of 食 (た) べる (to eat) which is used to describe the actual

state or condition of the subject; how to form: Verb て-form + いる]

小林一茶 Kobayashi Issa (1763 – 1828) [A Japanese poet and lay Buddhist priest. He is known

as simply Issa, a pen name which means "Cup-of-tea". He is regarded as one of the four

Haiku masters in Japan.]

JLPT N5 Kanji

男

On: ダン

Kun: おとこ

Meaning: man; male

Audio of Readings

The top part 田 means "rice field" and 力 means "power." So a **powerful man** works in the **rice field**.

Stroke Order:

男 丨 冂 田 用 田 甲 男

Examples:

だんじょ
男女 men and women

おとこ
男らしい manly, like a man

ゆきおとこ
雪男 the abominable snowman

Audio of Example

あか　　　　おとこ　　こ
赤ちゃんは 男 の子です。

akachan wa otoko no ko desu.

The baby is a boy.

Audio of Example

VOCABULARY:

赤ちゃん *akachan*—baby; infant

は *wa*—(indicates the sentence topic)

男の子 *otoko no ko*—boy; young man

です *desu*—be; is

くらい・ぐらい

About

ABOUT:

Approximate amount of something. ぐらい or くらい is used for asking "about how much" or "about how many." You can use it for estimating the number of things or time.

HOW TO USE:

- Place after the object you are estimating.
- It is used for estimating objects, time, and also as a pronoun.

EXAMPLES:

お客様は、どの<u>くらい</u>来ましたか？

<u>About</u> how many customers came?

[Here, くらい is used as an interrogative pronoun: *about how many*?]

Example 1

ええと、１００人<u>くらい</u>来ました。

Let me see, <u>**about**</u> 100 people came.

[Here, it estimates the number, "100 people."]

Example 2

Continued

<ruby>8時<rt>はちじ</rt></ruby>**ぐらい**に<ruby>始<rt>はじ</rt></ruby>まります。

It will begin **about** eight o'clock.

[Add に to show when it will begin.]

Example 3

MAIN POINTS:

■ くらい and ぐらい are interchangeable and mean the same thing.

VOCABULARY:

- お客様 *okyakusama*—visitor; customer; client

- は *wa*—(indicates the sentence topic)

- どのくらい *dono kurai*—how; how many; how much; how long; how far

- 来ました *kimashita*—came [polite past form of 来る (to come; to arrive)]

- か *ka*—(question marker)

- ええと *eeto*—let me see; well; errr ...; uhh ...

- 100人 *hyaku nin*—100 people [人 (person; people; counter for people)]

- くらい *kurai*—approximately; about; around

Vocabulary Continued

- 8時 *hachi ji*—eight o'clock

- ぐらい *gurai*—approximately; about; around; or so

- に *ni*—at [specifies time]

- 始まります *hajimarimasu*—to begin; to start [polite/ます form of 始まる (to begin)]

よんでみよう！ LET'S READ!

Learn through reading for (very) beginners of Japanese

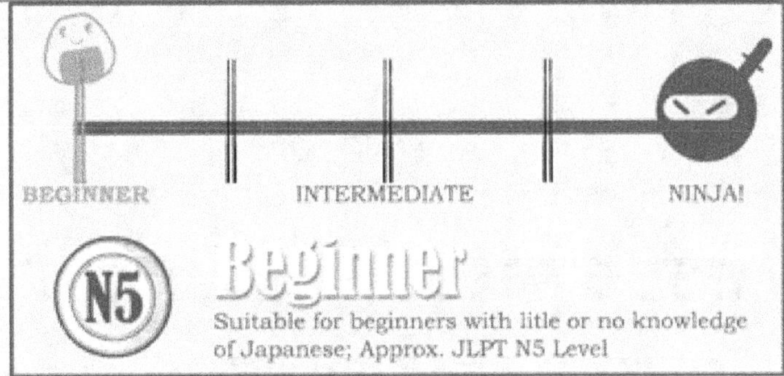

Have you only recently learned hiragana but need practice? Or perhaps, your hiragana is no problem, but you want to build your reading comprehension?

This segment is here to the rescue!

Read real Japanese—beginner level but not boring Japanese! Enjoy reading flash fiction, super short essays, and funny stories of common mistakes made by foreigners in Japan.

Best of all, the only requirement is that you can read hiragana. Vocabulary and grammar will be defined and explained.

The format is a little different from our other more advanced readers. The idea is for the reader to read the entire story three times. Each page will have a sentence or two in hiragana (with spaces between words for you to see "words" instead of syllables) at the top and that same content in full Japanese (with furigana) at the bottom. The middle will have the glossary and grammatical explanations. Lastly, the story will be presented in Japanese without furigana. See if you can read it after going through the explanations.

If you have just learned hiragana, you may want to listen to the sound file while reading the hiragana section to practice correct pronunciation. If you have studied Japanese a bit longer, you may want to start with the bottom version and take note of the glossary for understanding.

Makoto+ members can access this in a more interactive format. To learn more:

http://MakotoPlus.com

And now...

Let's learn about...

JAPANESE STREET FOOD
PART III: "MITARASHI DANGO"

Normal Speed

Slow Speed

Normal Speed

Slow Speed

日本のストリートフード　その3

「みたらし団子」

JAPANESE STREET FOOD, PART III

"MITARASHI DANGO"

こんかい　は、「みたらし　だんご」を　ごしょうかい　します。

GLOSSARY AND NOTES

日本のストリートフード *nihon no sutori-to fu-do*—street food in Japan; street food of Japan; Japanese street food [日本 (Japan) + の (of; in; 's; modifier) + ストリートフード (street food)]

その3 *sono san*—Part III

「みたらし団子」 「*mitarashi dango*」—"mitarashi dango" [「」 (quotation marks; " ") + みたらし団子 (*mitarashi dango*; skewered rice dumplings in a sweet soy glaze)]

今回は *konkai wa*—this time [今回 (this time; now) + は (adds emphasis)]

「みたらし団子」をご紹介します 「*mitarashi dango*」 *o goshoukai shimasu*— (we) will introduce "mitarashi dango" [「みたらし団子」 ("mitarashi dango") + を (indicates the direct object of action) + ご紹介します (let (me) introduce; introduce; ご (honorific/polite/humble prefix) + 紹介します (introduce; bring on; induct))]

今回は、「みたらし団子」をご紹介します。

にほん　の　すとりーと　ふーど　で　とても　ながい　れきし　が
あります。みたらし　だんご　は、ちいさな　まるい　だんご　です。
よん　こ　から　ご　こ、くし　に　さして　やきます。

GLOSSARY AND NOTES

日本のストリートフード *nihon no sutori-to fu-do*—street food in Japan; street food of Japan; Japanese street food

で *de*—(て-form of copula です (be; is) which is used to connect two or three sentences)

とても *totemo*—very; awfully; exceedingly

長い *nagai*—long (distance, length)

歴史 *rekishi*—history

(が) あります　*(ga) arimasu*—there is (non-living things) [how to form: Noun + (が)あります]

「みたらし団子」　「*mitarashi dango*」—"mitarashi dango"

は *wa*—(indicates the sentence topic)

小さな *chiisana*—small; little; tiny

丸い *marui*—round; circular; spherical

団子 *dango*—*dango*; dumpling (usually sweet)

です *desu*—be; is

4個から5個 *yon ko kara go ko*—4pcs to 5pcs [4個 (4pcs; 個 (counter for articles)) + から (from) + 5個 (5 pcs)]

串にさして焼きます *kushi ni sashite yakimasu*—grilled on a skewer; roast (dumplings) on skewer [串 (spit; skewer) + に (on) + さして (て-form of さす (to pierce; to stick; to thrust) which is used to connect to the next verb 焼きます) + 焼きます (polite/ます form of 焼く (to roast; to grill; to barbecue))]

日本のストリートフードでとても長い歴史があります。みたら
し団子は、小さな丸い団子です。 4個から5個、串にさして焼
きます。

それ　から、あまからい　たれ　を　かけます。とても　おいしい　です　よ。みたらし　だんご　は　きょうと　で　はじまりました。きょうと　の　ある　まつり　で　みたらし　だんご　が　とても　ゆうめい　に　なりました。

GLOSSARY AND NOTES

それから *sore kara*—and then; after that

甘辛いたれをかけます *amakarai tare o kakemasu*—top with a sweet and spicy sauce [甘辛いたれ (sweet and spicy sauce; salty-sweet sauce) + を (indicates the direct object of action) + かけます (polite/ます form of かける (to put on top of; to spread; to cover))]

とてもおいしい *totemo oishii*—very delicious [とても (very) + おいしい (good(-tasting); delicious; tasty)]

ですよ *desu yo*—(sentence ender showing assertion or confidence)

京都で始まりました *kyouto de hajimarimashita*—originated in Kyoto [京都 (Kyoto (city, prefecture)) + で (in; at; indicates the location of action) + 始まりました (originated; polite past form of 始まる (to originate; to begin; to start))]

京都のある祭りで *kyouto no aru matsuri de*—at a festival in Kyoto [京都 (Kyoto (city, prefecture)) + の (of; modifier) + ある (to exist; is used to indicate the existence of inanimate objects) + 祭り (festival; feast) + で (at; indicates the location of action)]

が *ga*—(identifies what performs the action; emphasizes the preceding word みたらし団子 (*mitarashi dango*))

とても有名になりました *totemo yuumei ni narimashita*—became very famous [とても (very; awfully; exceedingly) + 有名 (famous) + に (expresses the result of change) + なりました (became; polite past form of なる (to become; to reach))]

それから、甘辛いたれをかけます。とてもおいしいですよ。みたらし団子は京都で始まりました。京都のある祭りでみたらし団子がとても有名になりました。

この　まつり　は　へいあん　じだい　から　あります。みたらし
だんご　も　せん　ねん　いじょう　の　れきし　が　ある　こと
に　なります。「みたらし　だんご」にほん　に　きたら、ぜひ　た
べて　みて　ください。

GLOSSARY AND NOTES

この祭りは *kono matsuri wa*—this festival [この　(this) + 祭り　(festival; feast) + は　(indicates the sentence topic)]

平安時代からあります *heian jidai kara arimasu*—has been around since the Heian period (794 - 1185) [平安時代　(Heian period (794-1185)) + から　(from; since) + あります　(polite/ます　form of ある　(to exist; to be))]

も　*mo*—(emphasizes the preceding word みたらし団子　(*mitarashi dango*))

千年以上の歴史がある　*sen nen ijou no rekishi ga aru*—have a history of more than 1,000 years [千年　(millennium; one thousand years; 千　(1,000; thousand) + 年　(year)) + 以上　(... and over; ... and above; ... and upwards; ... or more) + の　(of; modifier) + 歴史　(history) + が　(identifies what performs the action; emphasizes the preceding word) + ある　(to have; to be; to exist)]

ことになります　*koto ni narimasu*—it turns out that ... [how to form: Verb (dictionary form) + ことになります]

日本に来たら　*nihon ni kitara*—if (you) come to Japan [日本　(Japan) + に　(to; expresses the direction and destination) + 来たら　(from 来る　(to come; plain form is "ku" but changes to "ki" when conjugated); ~たら　means "when ~; if; after"; how to form: Verb (た　form) + ら)]

ぜひ　*zehi*—certainly; without fail; please; definitely

食べてみてください　*tabete mite kudasai*—please try to eat (*mitarashi dango*); you must try (*mitarashi dango*) [from 食べる　(to eat); ~てみてください　is used to express a demand, suggestion to someone to do something for the first time; how to form: Verb て-form + みてください]

この祭りは平安時代からあります。みたらし団子も千年以上の
歴史があることになります。「みたらし団子」日本に来たら、
ぜひ食べてみてください。

27

日本のストリートフード　その３
「みたらし団子」
JAPANESE STREET FOOD , PART III
"MITARASHI DANGO "

Now, let's read the story once more in natural Japanese.
Lastly, check the English translation to make sure you understand.

　今回は、「みたらし団子」をご紹介します。日本のストリートフードでとても長い歴史があります。みたらし団子は、小さな丸い団子です。4個から5個、串にさして焼きます。それから、甘辛いたれをかけます。とてもおいしいですよ。みたらし団子は京都で始まりました。京都のある祭りでみたらし団子がとても有名になりました。この祭りは平安時代からあります。みたらし団子も千年以上の歴史があることになります。「みたらし団子」日本に来たら、ぜひ食べてみてください。

ENGLISH: (try to save this for last)

　This time, we will introduce "Mitarashi Dango". It is a Japanese street food with a very long history. *Mitarashi dango* are small round dumplings, consisting of four to five dumplings, grilled on a skewer. Then, they are topped with a sweet and spicy sauce. They are very delicious. *Mitarashi dango* originated in Kyoto. *Mitarashi dango* became very famous at a festival in Kyoto. This festival has been around since the Heian period (794-1185). *Mitarashi dango* have a history of more than 1,000 years. If you come to Japan, you must try "Mitarashi Dango".

KEY VOCABULARY

日本のストリートフード *nihon no sutori-to fu-do*—street food in Japan; Japanese street food

みたらし団子 *mitarashi dango*—mitarashi dango; skewered rice dumplings in a sweet soy glaze

団子 *dango*—dango; dumpling (usually sweet)

歴史 *rekishi*—history

甘辛いたれ *amakarai tare*—sweet and spicy sauce

丸い *marui*—round; circular

串にさして焼きます *kushi ni sashite yakimasu*—grilled on a skewer

とてもおいしい *totemo oishii*—very delicious

祭り *matsuri*—festival

JAPANESE READER

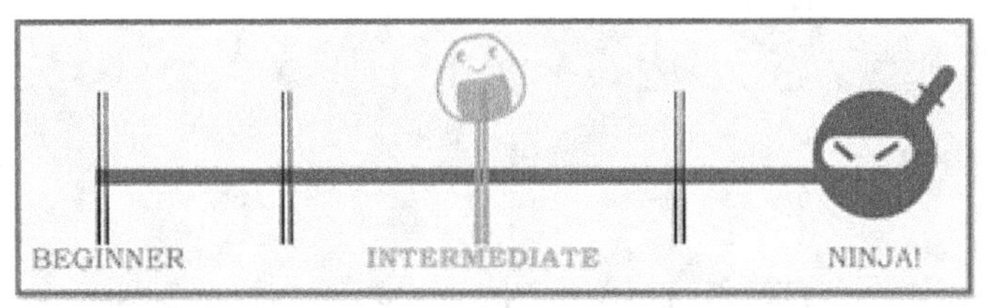

きっちょむさんの馬

Kicchomu's Horse

Story Read Normal

Story Read Slow Speed

むかしむかし、きっちょむさんという面白い人がいました。ある日、きっちょむさんは、馬を川で洗おうと思って、馬を川に連れて行きました。

きっちょむさんの馬 Kicchomu's horse [きっちょむさん (Kicchomu; さん is an honorific suffix which means Mr., Mrs., or Miss that can be used with both first and last names and both genders) + の (of; 's; modifier) + 馬 (horse)]

むかしむかし long ago; once upon a time

きっちょむさんというnamed Kicchomu [きっちょむさん (Kicchomu) + という (named; is used to define, describe, and generally just talk about the thing itself)]

面白い人 interesting man [面白い (interesting; fascinating; enthralling) + 人 (man; person; people)]

(が)いました there was/were [polite past form of (が)いる (there is/are; to be (living things)); how to form: Noun + (が)いました]

ある日 one day; (on) a certain day [ある (a certain; some) + 日 (day)]

は (indicates the sentence topic)

馬 horse

を (indicates the direct object of action)

川で at the river [川 (river; stream) + で (in; at; indicates the location of action)]

洗おうと思って thinking to wash [洗おう (plain volitional form of 洗う (to wash; to cleanse) which is used when the speaker initiates an act) + と思って (て-form of と思う (to think...; I think...; you think...) which is used to connect to the next phrase)]

馬を川に連れて行きました took the horse to the river [馬 (horse) + を (indicates the direct object of action) + 川 (river; stream) + に (to; expresses the direction and destination) + 連れて行きました (polite past form of 連れて行く (to take (someone; to a place); to take (someone) with one; to take along))]

川には、隣の奥さんが洗濯に来ていました。きっちょむさん

は、いたずらを思いつきました。 懐に持っていた小銭をひと

つかみだして、そっと馬のお尻の穴をさすりました。

川には to the river [川 (river; stream) + に (to; expresses the destination) + は (adds emphasis)]

隣の奥さんが the neighbor's wife [隣 (next-door
neighbor; next (to); adjoining) + の (of; 's; modifier) +
奥さん (wife; your wife; his wife; married lady) + が
(identifies who performs the action; emphasizes the
preceding word)]

洗濯に来ていました had come to do the laundry; came
for laundry [洗濯 (washing; laundry) + に (for
(purpose)) + 来ていました (had come; ていました
form of 来る (to come; to arrive))]

いたずらを思いつきました came up with a mischievous idea [いたずら (mischief; prank; trick) + を
(indicates the direct object of action) + 思いつきまし
た (polite past form of 思いつく (to think of; to hit
upon; to come into one's mind; to be struck with an
idea))]

懐に in (his) pocket [懐 (inside the breast of one's
clothing (especially *kimono*); pocket) + に (in; indicates the location of existence)]

持っていた had [plain past form of 持っている (hold;
have; possess; ている form of 持つ (to hold (in one's
hand); to take; to carry; to have) which is used to describe the actual state or condition of the subject)]

小銭をひとつかみだして take out a handful of coins
and [小銭 (small change; coins) + を (indicates 小銭
as the direct object of action) + ひとつかみ (handful)
+ だして (て-form of だす (to take out; to put out)
which is used to connect to the next phrase)]

そっと softly; gently

馬のお尻の穴をさすりました rubbed the horse's butt
hole [馬 (horse) + の ('s; of) + お尻 (butt; bottom;
buttocks) + の (of; modifier) + 穴 (hole) + を
(indicates the direct object of action) + さすりました
(rubbed; polite past form of さする (to rub; to pat; to
massage))]

すると、馬は糞をしました。それをざるで受けたきっちょむさん
は、その中に小銭を入れました。そして、川の水で馬の糞を洗う
と、まるで糞の中から、小銭が出てきたように見えました。

すると then; and

馬は糞をしました the horse pooped [馬 (horse) + は
(indicates the sentence topic) + 糞をしました
(pooped; polite past form of 糞をする (have a bowel
movement; poop))]

それをざるで (caught) it with a sieve [それ (that; it) +
を (indicates the direct object of action) + ざる
(draining basket (traditionally made of bamboo); col-
ander; strainer; sieve) + で (with; indicates means of
action)]

受けた caught [plain past form of 受ける (to catch; to
receive; to get)]

その中に in it; inside it [その (that; the; it) + 中 (in;
inside) + に (expresses the location of existence)]

小銭を入れました put coins (in it) [小銭 (small change;
coins) + を (indicates 小銭 as the direct object of action) + 入れました (put; polite past form of 入れる (to
put in; to let in))]

そして and; then

川の水で with river water [川 (river; stream) + の (of;
‘s; modifier) + 水 (water) + で (with; indicates
means of action)]

馬の糞を洗うと when (he) washed the horse’s feces [
馬 (horse) + の (‘s; of; modifier) + 糞 (feces; poop)
+ を (indicates the direct object of action) + 洗う (to
wash; to cleanse) + と (when)]

まるで as if; as though; just like

糞の中から (came out) of the feces [糞 (feces; poop) +
の (of; modifier) + 中 (of the; out of; in) + から
(from)]

小銭が出てきた coins came out [小銭 (small change;
coins) + が (emphasizes the preceding word 小銭;
identifies what performs the action) + 出てきた
(came out; plain past form of 出てくる (to come
out; to appear))]

ように ... looks/seems/sounds/feels like ...

見えました looked [polite past form of 見える (to
look; to seem; to appear)]

隣 の奥さんはびっくりしてきっちょむさんに言いました。

「あれま、その馬は銭の糞をするのかね？」

「そうじゃ、お前さんの見たとおりだよ。」

隣の奥さんは the neighbor's wife [隣 (neighboring house; next (to); adjoining; adjacent) + の ('s; of; modifier) + 奥さん (wife; married lady) + は (indicates the sentence topic)]

びっくりして astonished and [て-form of びっくりする (feel astonished; get a surprise) which is used to connect to the next phrase]

きっちょむさんに言いました told Kicchomu [きっちょむさん (Kicchomu) + に (expresses the object of the verb) + 言いました (told; polite past form of 言う (to tell; to say; to utter))]

「」 (quotation marks; " ")

あれま oh my!; my goodness!

その馬は that horse [その (that; the) + 馬 (horse) + は (indicates the sentence topic)]

銭の糞をする (that horse) poops coins [銭 (round coin with a (square) hole in the center; money) + の (of; modifier) + 糞 (feces (especially animal); poop) + を (indicates the direct object of action) + する (to do)]

の (explanatory particle)

かね (interrogative sentence-ending particle expressing doubt)

そうじゃ that's right; yes

お前さんの見たとおり as you saw (it) [お前さん (you) + の (modifier) + 見たとおり (as (you) saw; ~とおり means "as; in the way; in the same way as"; how to form: Verb-casual, past + とおり)]

だよ (sentence ender showing assertion or confidence) [is used in spoken Japanese and informal situations]

隣の奥さんは、洗濯物を放り出して、村に行ってこのことをみんなに話しました。すると、たくさんの村の人が馬を見にやってきました。「きっちょむさん、銭の糞をするという馬はそれかね。よく見せておくれ。」

隣の奥さん neighbor's wife

洗濯物を放り出して (the neighbor's wife) abandoned her laundry and [洗濯物 (laundry; the washing) + を (indicates the direct object of action) + 放り出して (て-form of 放り出す (to abandon; to throw out) which is used to connect to the next phrase, creating the meaning of "and")]

村に行って went to the village [村 (village) + に (to; expresses the direction and destination) + 行って (て-form of 行く (to go) which is used to connect to the next phrase)]

このこと this; this thing [この (this) + こと (thing; matter)]

みんなに話しました told everyone [みんな (everyone; everybody; all) + に (expresses the object of the verb) + 話しました (told; polite past form of 話す (to talk; to tell))]

すると then; and then; and

たくさんの村の人が many villagers [たくさん (a lot; lots; plenty; many) + の (modifier) + 村 (village) + の (of; modifier) + 人 (person; people) + が (identifies who performs the action)]

馬を見にやってきました came to see the horse [馬 (horse) + を (indicates the direct object of action) + 見にやってきました (came to see; 「verb stem + にやってきました」 means "come to (do something)")]

銭の糞をする poop coins [銭 (coin; money) + の (of; modifier) + 糞をする (poop; leave one's excrement)]

という馬は the horse that (poops coins) [という (that) + 馬 (horse) + は (indicates the sentence topic)]

それ that; it

かね (interrogative sentence-ending particle expressing doubt)

よく well; properly

見せておくれ show (us) [from 見せる (to show; to display); ~ておくれ is the "softened" form of the ~てくれる-form (do something for someone), which is used as an imperative; how to form: Verb (て form) + おくれ]

きっちょむさんは、またこっそりと小銭を馬の糞に混ぜて、川で洗ってみんなに見せました。「ほほ〜、この馬は銭の糞をするんだなぁ〜。」たちまち村中の評判になりました。

また again; once more

こっそりと secretly [こっそり (secretly; in secret) + と (is used with sound words, and can be used after onomatopoeic adverbs)]

小銭を馬の糞に混ぜて mix some coins into the horse's feces [小銭 (small change; coins) + を (indicates the direct object of action) + 馬 (horse) + の ('s; modifier) + 糞 (feces; excrement; poop) + に (into) + 混ぜて (て-form of 混ぜる (to mix; to stir) which is used to connect to the next phrase)]

川で洗って wash in the river and [川 (river; stream) + で (in; indicates the location of action) + 洗って (て-form of 洗う (to wash; to cleanse; to rinse) which is used to connect to the next phrase, creating the meaning of "and")]

みんなに見せました showed to everyone [みんな (everyone; everybody; all) + に (to) + 見せました (showed; polite past form of 見せる (to show; to display))]

ほほ〜 ho-ho

この馬は this horse [この (this) + 馬 (horse) + は (indicates the sentence topic)]

銭の糞をする poop coins [銭 (coin; money) + の (of; modifier) + 糞をする(poop; leave one's excrement)]

んだ (shows emphasis) [indicates that the statement being made is based on background information]

なぁ〜 (casual suffix) [is used when you express your opinion or feeling]

たちまち in an instant; in a moment; immediately

村中の評判になりました became popular throughout the village [村 (village) + 中 (throughout) + の (of; modifier) + 評判 (reputation; (public) estimation; popularity) + に (expresses the result of change) + なりました (became; polite past form of なる (to become; to turn))]

そして、お金持ちの庄屋さんもこの話を聞きました。庄屋さん

は、お金をたっぷり持ってきっちょむさんの家にやってきまし

た。「きっちゃむさん、その馬を売ってくれないか？10両出

そう。」

そして and; and then

お金持ちの庄屋さんも the rich village headman also
[お金持ち (rich person; rich) + の (of; modifier) +
庄屋さん (village headman (especially in the Kansai
region)) + も (also; too)]

この話を聞きました heard this story [この (this) +
話 (tale; story) + を (indicates the direct object of
action) + 聞きました (heard; polite past form of 聞く
(to hear; to listen))]

お金をたっぷり持って bring plenty of money [お金
(money) + を (indicates the direct object of action) +
たっぷり (full; in plenty) + 持って (て-form of 持つ
(to hold (in one's hand); to take; to carry) which is
used to connect to the next phrase)]

きっちょむさんの家にやってきました came to
Kicchomu's house [きっちょむさん (Kicchomu) +
の ('s; of; modifier) + 家 (house; residence; dwelling) + に (to; expresses the direction and destination) + やってきました (came; polite past form of
やってくる (to come along; to come around; to
come))]

その馬を売ってくれないか would you be willing to
sell me that horse [その (that; the) + 馬 (horse) +
を (indicates the direct object of action) + 売ってく
れないか (from 売る (to sell); ~てくれないか is
used to ask someone to do something for you polite-
ly; how to form: Verb て-form + くれないか)]

10両 ten *ryou* [両 (*ryou*; pre-Meiji unit of currency)

出そう will pay; will draw out (money)

きっちょむさんは、しめしめと思いましたが、わざと渋い顔を

して言いました。「この馬は、銭の糞をする大切な馬だから、

庄屋さんにいくらお金を積まれても売らない。」

しめしめと思いましたが "I got him now", (Kicchomu) thought but [しめしめ (that's it!; good!; I've got it!; I've done it!; bingo!) + と (used for quoting (thoughts, speech, etc.)) + 思いました (thought; polite past form of 思う (to think; to consider)) + が (but; however)]

わざと on purpose; deliberately; intentionally

渋い顔をして言いました made a reluctant face and said [渋い (sour (look); glum; grim; sullen) + 顔 (face; look) + を (indicates the direct object of action) + して (て-form of する (to do) which is used to connect to the next phrase, creating the meaning of "and") + 言いました (said; polite past form of 言う (to say; to utter))]

この馬は this horse [この (this) + 馬 (horse) + は (indicates the sentence topic)]

銭の糞をする (the horse that) poops money [銭 (coin; money) + の (of; modifier) + 糞 (feces; poop) + を (indicates the direct object of action) + する (to do)]

大切な馬 an important horse [大切な (important; significant; precious; valuable) + 馬 (horse)]

だから so; therefore; accordingly; consequently

庄屋さんに to the village headman [庄屋さん (village headman (especially in the Kansai region)) + に (to)]

いくらお金を積まれても売らない no matter how much money (you pay me), (I) will not sell (it) [いくら (no matter how; how much) + お金 (money) + を (indicates the direct object of action) + 積まれても も (from 積む (to accumulate; to load; to pile up); ～ても means "even; even if; even though ～"; how to form: Verb (て form) + も) + 売らない (do not sell; plain negative form of 売る (to sell)); いくら～ても means "no matter how ～"; how to form: いくら + Verb (て form) + も]

「いやいや、そんなことを言わないで売っておくれよ。 じゃあ、

２０両ではどうだい？」「う〜ん、もったいないなぁ。」「

３０両では？」「う〜ん、もう一息。」「うう、わかった。

いやいや no!; no no!; shaking head in refusal (like a child)

そんなこと such a thing [そんな (such; that sort of; that kind of; like that) + こと (thing; matter)]

そんなことを言わないで don't say that; do not say such a thing [そんなこと (such a thing) + を (indicates the direct object of action) + 言わないで (from 言う (to say; to utter); ~ないで means "without doing...; don't"; how to form: Verb (ない form) + で)]

売っておくれ sell (it) to me [from 売る (to sell); ~ておくれ is the "softened" form of the てくれる-form (do something for someone), which is used as an imperative]

よ (sentence ender showing emphasis and certainty)

じゃあ then; well; so

20両では 20 *ryou* [両 (*ryou*; pre-Meiji unit of currency) + で (indicates a total or an extent; is placed after a quantity, time, or amount of money) + は (adds emphasis)]

どう how; in what way; how about

だい (strong masculine sentence ending for asking questions)

う〜ん hmmm; well

もったいない wasteful; a waste

なぁ (casual suffix) [is used when you express your opinion or feeling; is generally considered to be "male speech"]

もう一息 just one more effort [もう (further; more; again) + 一息 (one breath; pause; break)]

うう uh; hmmm; huh

わかった okay; all right

ごじゅうりょう
５０両ならどうじゃ？」「よし、それなら売ろう。あとで金を

かえ　もんく　い　　　　　　　　い　　　　　うま
返せと文句を言うなよ。」そう言って、きっちょむさんは、馬

しょうや　　わた
を庄屋さんに渡しました。

50両ならどうじゃ how about 50 *ryou* [50 両 (50 *ryou*) + なら (if; in case) + どう (how; in what way; how about) + じゃ (plain copula; combination of で and は, which is used when talking about situation or condition)]

よし alright; all right; right on; looking good; OK; okay

それなら売ろう I'll sell (it) then [それなら (then; in that case) + 売ろう (I'll sell; plain volitional form of 売る (to sell) which is used when the speaker initiates an act)]

あとで later on; afterwards

金を返せ return (my) money [金 (money) + を (indicates 金 as the direct object of action) + 返せ (plain imperative form of 返す (return; give back))]

と (used for quoting (thoughts, speech, etc.))

文句を言うな don't complain [文句 (complaint; grumbling; objection) + を (indicates the direct object of action) + 言う (say; talk; complain) + な (don't ~; is used to order somebody to not do something; how to form: Verb (dictionary form) + な)]

よ (sentence ender showing emphasis and certainty)

そう言って having said that [そう (in that way; thus; such) + 言って (て-form of 言う (to say; to utter) which is used to connect to the next phrase)]

馬を庄屋さんに渡しました (Kicchomu) handed (his) horse to the village headman [馬 (horse) + を (indicates the direct object of action) + 庄屋さん (village headman) + に (to) + 渡しました (handed; polite past form of 渡す (to hand in; to pass; to give))]

庄屋さんは、お金を払って嬉しそうに馬を連れて家に帰りまし
た。しばらくして庄屋さんは、かんかんに怒ってきっちょむさ
んのところにやってきました。「きっちょむさん、この馬は
ちっとも銭の糞などしないじゃないか？

庄屋さんは the village headman [庄屋さん (village headman) + は (indicates the sentence topic)]

お金を払って pay the money and [お金 (money) + を (indicates the direct object of action) + 払って (て-form of 払う (to pay) which is used to connect to the next phrase, creating the meaning of "and")]

嬉しそうに happily; joyfully; delightedly; joyously

馬を連れて take the horse [馬 (horse) + を (indicates the direct object of action) + 連れて (て-form of 連れる (to take along; to go with) which is used to connect to the next phrase)]

家に帰りました went home [家 (house; residence; dwelling) + に (expresses the direction and destination) + 帰りました (polite past form of 帰る (to return; to come home; to go back))]

しばらくして after a short time; presently

かんかんに怒って get furious and [かんかんに (extreme anger; fury; rage) + 怒って (て-form of 怒る (to get angry; to get mad) which is used to connect to the next phrase, creating the meaning of "and")]

きっちょむさんのところに came to Kicchomu; came to Kicchomu's place [きっちょむさん (Kicchomu) + の ('s; indicates possessive) + ところ (place; site) + に (to; expresses the direction and destination)]

やってきました came; came around [polite past form of やってくる (to come along; to come around; to turn up)]

この馬は this horse [この (this) + 馬 (horse) + は (indicates the sentence topic)]

ちっとも (not) at all; (not) a bit; (not) in the least

銭の糞などしないじゃないか (this horse) doesn't poop coins, etc., doesn't it? [銭 (coin; money) + の (of; modifier) + 糞 (feces; excrement; dung) + など (et cetera; etc.; and the like; and so forth) + しない (don't; doesn't; plain negative form of する (to do)) + じゃないか (isn't it?; doesn't it?)]

馬を返すから、お金を返してくれ！！」「あとで金を返せと言うなといっただろう？銭の糞をしない？庄屋さんは馬に何を食べさせているんだい？」「それは、馬の食べるものじゃ。

馬を返す return the horse [馬 (horse) + を (indicates the direct object of action) + 返す (to return (something); to restore; to give back)]

から so; because; since

お金を返してくれ (you) give me back my money [お金 (money) + を (indicates the direct object of action) + 返してくれ (give me back; ~てくれ is used to ask someone to do something; how to form: Verb て-form + くれ)]

あとで later on; afterwards

金を返せと言うなといった (I) told (you) not to ask for your money back [金 (money) + を (indicates 金 as the direct object of action) + 返せ (plain imperative form of 返す (return; give back)) + と (used for quoting (thoughts, speech, etc.)) + 言う (to say; to utter; to talk) + な (don't ~; is used to order somebody to not do something; how to form: Verb (dictionary form) + な) + といった (told; plain past form of という (is used when we quote what somebody has said))]

だろう right?; don't you agree?

銭の糞をしない do not poop coins [銭 (coin; money) + の (of; modifier) + 糞 (poop; feces) + を (indicates the direct object of action) + しない (don't; plain negative form of する (to do))]

馬に to the horse [馬 (horse) + に (to)]

何を食べさせている what do (you) feed (to the horse); what are (you) feeding [何 (what) + を (indicates the direct object of action) + 食べさせて いる (ている form of 食べさせる (plain causative positive form of 食べる (to eat)) which is used to express one's habitual actions; how to form: Verb て-form + いる)]

んだい (turns a sentence into a question (casual form))

それは that is

馬の食べるものじゃ what horses eat [馬 (horse) + の ('s; of; modifier) + 食べるもの (food; what (the horse) eats) + じゃ (is used to mean だ (casual form of the polite copula です (be; is); is used to affirm and emphasize your sentence))]

草とか、麦とか豆とか。」「ああ、それじゃだめだ。銭の糞を

させるなら、銭を食べさせなきゃいけない。当たり前だろう

が。」庄屋さんは、口をぽかんと開けて何も言えなかったそう

です。おしまい。

草 grass; weed; herb

麦 wheat; barley; oat (oats)

豆 legume (especially edible legumes or their seeds, e.g. beans, peas, pulses)

とか and/or [connecting particle which is used to list the same kind of multiple things and imply there are other items that could be included in the list]

ああ ah!; oh!

それじゃだめだ that's not any good; it doesn't work like that; that's not going to work

銭の糞をさせるなら if (you) want (the horse) to poop coins; if (you) let the horse poop coins [銭 (coin; money) + の (of; modifier) + 糞 (poop; feces) + を (indicates the direct object of action) + させる (causative form of する (to do); to make/let somebody do something) + なら (if; in case; if it is the case that)]

銭を食べさせなきゃいけない you have to feed (him) coins [銭 (coin; money) + を (indicates the direct object of action) + 食べさせなきゃいけない (have to feed; ~なきゃいけない (casual form) means "must; have to" which is used to tell yourself (or other peo-ple) what you have to do; how to form: Verb ない form (remove い) + きゃいけない)]

当たり前 common sense; natural; reasonable; obvious

だろう will no doubt; might well; should; would

が (merely used as a softener without any implication of contrast or opposition)

口をぽかんと開けて (the village headman) with (his) mouth hanging open [口 (mouth) + を (indicates the direct object of action) + ぽかん (openmouthed; with one's mouth wide-open) + と (is used after the adverb ぽかん) + 開けて (て-form of 開ける (to open) which is used to connect to the next phrase)]

何も言えなかった could not say anything [何も ((not) anything; (nothing) at all; (not) any; nothing) + 言えなかった (could not say; plain potential negative past form of 言う (to say; to utter))]

そうです it seems; it appears that; I hear that...

おしまい the end

Kicchomu's Horse

Please try to tackle the Japanese first and use this only as needed.

Once upon a time, there was an interesting man named Kicchomu. One day, Kicchomu decided to take his horse to the river to wash it.

The neighbor's wife had come to the river to do the laundry. Kicchomu came up with a mischievous idea. He took a handful of coins from his pocket and gently rubbed the horse's butt hole. Then the horse pooped. Kicchomu caught it with a sieve basket and put some coins in it. And when he washed the horse's feces with river water, it looked as if coins came out of the feces.

The neighbor's wife was astonished and told Kicchomu: "Oh my, does that horse poop coins?"

"Yes, just as you saw it."

The neighbor's wife abandoned her laundry and went to the village to tell everyone about this. Then many villagers came to see the horse.

"Kicchomu, is that the horse that poops coins? Show us."

Kicchomu again secretly mixed some coins into the horse's feces, washed it in the river, and showed it to everyone.

"Ho-ho-ho, this horse poops coins!"

It immediately became popular throughout the village. And the rich village headman also heard about this story. The village headman came to Kicchomu's house with plenty of money.

"Kicchomu, would you be willing to sell me that horse for ten ryou?"

"I got him now", Kicchomu thought but he deliberately made a reluctant face and said, "This horse is an important horse that poops money, so no matter how much money you pay me, I will not sell it."

"No, no, don't say that, just sell it to me. How about 20 ryou then?"

"Hmmm, what a waste."

"How about 30 ryou?"

"Ummm, getting close."

"Uh, okay, how about 50 ryou?"

"All right, I'll sell it then. Don't complain about getting your money back later on."

Continued

Having said that, Kicchomu handed the horse to the village headman. The village headman paid the money and happily took the horse home.

After a while, the village headman got furious and came to Kicchomu.

"Kicchomu, this horse doesn't poop coins at all, doesn't it? I'll give you back your horse, so you give me back my money!"

"I told you not to ask for your money back later on, right? Not pooping coins? What do you feed to the horse?"

"That's what horses eat. Grass, wheat, legumes..."

"Oh, that's not any good. If you want him to poop coins, you have to feed him coins. That's just common sense."

The village headman, with his mouth hanging open, could not say anything.

The end.

きっちょむさんの馬

　むかしむかし、きっちょむさんという面白い人がいました。ある日、きっちょむさんは、馬を川で洗おうと思って、馬を川に連れて行きました。

　川には、隣の奥さんが洗濯に来ていました。きっちょむさんは、いたずらを思いつきました。懐に持っていた小銭をひとつかみだして、そっと馬のお尻の穴をさすりました。すると、馬は糞をしました。それをざるで受けたきっちょむさんは、その中に小銭を入れました。そして、川の水で馬の糞を洗うと、まるで糞の中から、小銭が出てきたように見えました。

　隣の奥さんはびっくりしてきっちょむさんに言いました。「あれま、その馬は銭の糞をするのかね？」

　「そうじゃ、お前さんの見たとおりだよ。」

　隣の奥さんは、洗濯物を放り出して、村に行ってこのことをみんなに話しました。すると、たくさんの村の人が馬を見にやってきました。

　「きっちょむさん、銭の糞をするという馬はそれかね。よく見せておくれ。」
きっちょむさんは、またこっそりと小銭を馬の糞に混ぜて、川で洗ってみんなに見せました。「ほほ〜、この馬は銭の糞をするんだなぁ〜。」

　たちまち村中の評判になりました。そして、お金持ちの庄屋さんもこの話を聞きました。庄屋さんは、お金をたっぷり持ってきっちょむさんの家にやってきました。

　「きっちゃむさん、その馬を売ってくれないか？10両出そう。」

　きっちょむさんは、しめしめと思いましたが、わざと渋い顔をして言いました。「この馬は、銭の糞をする大切な馬だから、庄屋さんにいくらお金を積まれても売らない。」

Continued

「いやいや、そんなことを言わないで売っておくれよ。じゃあ、20両ではどうだい？」

「う〜ん、もったいないなぁ。」

「30両では？」

「う〜ん、もう一息。」

「うう、わかった。50両ならどうじゃ？」

「よし、それなら売ろう。あとで金を返せと文句を言うなよ。」そう言って、きっちょむさんは、馬を庄屋さんに渡しました。庄屋さんは、お金を払って嬉しそうに馬を連れて家に帰りました。

　しばらくして庄屋さんは、かんかんに怒ってきっちょむさんのところにやってきました。

「きっちょむさん、この馬はちっとも銭の糞などしないじゃないか？馬を返すから、お金を返してくれ！！」

　「あとで金を返せと言うなと言っただろう？銭の糞をしない？庄屋さんは馬に何を食べさせているんだい？」

　「それは、馬の食べるものじゃ。草とか、麦とか豆とか。」

　「ああ、それじゃだめだ。銭の糞をさせるなら、銭を食べさせなきゃいけない。当たり前だろうが。」

　庄屋さんは、口をぽかんと開けて何も言えなかったそうです。

　おしまい。

Kanji in Focus

It is usually helpful to create a story based on the meanings of the kanji parts. Often, different kanji learning systems will use different "meanings" for the parts. We try to give the most common ones, but consistency is best. Choose one meaning per kanji part and stick with it. The following are a selection of the kanji found in this story. The <u>underlined</u> reading is probably the most used.

隣	READINGS / MEANING / EXAMPLE	リン・<u>となり</u> neighboring きんりん 近隣 neighborhood; vicinity	阝 town; place; hill; dam 米 rice; USA 舛 dancing; dancing legs Our *neighboring* **town** 阝 is celebrating a **rice** 米 festival with street **dancing** 舛 in colorful costumes.
奥	READINGS / MEANING / EXAMPLE	オウ・<u>おく</u>・おくまる heart; interior おく 奥さん wife; your wife; his wife; married lady	丶 dot 冂 upside-down box 米 rice; USA; meter 大 large; big; great; huge The **dot** 丶 on top of the **upside-down box** 冂 is a guide for loading **rice** 米 sacks into the *interior* part of the **huge** 大 warehouse.
懐	READINGS / MEANING / EXAMPLE	カイ・エ・<u>ふところ</u>・<u>なつかしい</u>・なつかしむ・なつく・なつける・なずける・いだく・おもう pocket; feelings; heart; yearn ふところ 懐 pocket; bosom	忄 heart 十 ten; 10 罒 net 衣 clothes; garment Her **heart** 忄 *yearns* for **ten** 十 kinds of **net** 罒 **garment** 衣.
洗	READINGS / MEANING / EXAMPLE	<u>セン</u>・<u>あらう</u> wash; inquire into あら 洗う to wash; to cleanse	氵 water 先 point; tip; end *Wash* thoroughly with **water** 氵 to clean the **tip** 先 of the knife.
評	READINGS / MEANING / EXAMPLE	<u>ヒョウ</u> evaluate; criticism; comment ひょうばん 評判 reputation; fame; (public) estimation	言 word; remark; statement 平 something broad and flat They *evaluate* his **statement** 言 about **something broad and flat** 平.

Kanji in Focus Continued

糞	**READINGS** **MEANING** **EXAMPLE**	フン・くそ feces; excrement ふん 糞 feces (especially animal); excrement; dung	米 rice; USA 田 rice field 艹 grass; herb; plant 一 one; 1 八 eight; legs Using fertilizer from animal *feces* and dried **rice** 米, for **rice field** 田 and **herb** 艹 plantation, is **one** 一 out of **eight** 八 methods of organic farming.
持	**READINGS** **MEANING** **EXAMPLE**	ジ・もつ・~もち・もてる hold; have かねも お金持ち rich person; rich	扌 hand 土 soil, earth, ground 寸 length; measurement With your bare **hands** 扌, can you *hold* the **earth** 土 and tell its **measurement** 寸?
両	**READINGS** **MEANING** **EXAMPLE**	リョウ・てる・ふたつ both; old Japanese coin りょうしん 両親 parents; both parents	一 one; 1 冂 upside-down box 丨 line; vertical stroke; rod 山 mountain; hill I found **one** 一 *old Japanese coin* in an **upside-down box** 冂 beside a **rod** 丨 on the **mountain** 山 top.
積	**READINGS** **MEANING** **EXAMPLE**	セキ・つむ・~づみ・つもる・つもり pile up; stack; load; volume るいせき 累積 accumulation	禾 two-branch tree 主 lord, chief, master 貝 shellfish; seashell; shell They *pile up* stones under a **two-branch tree** 禾 near the mansion of the **master** 主 of **seashells** 貝 handicraft.
銭	**READINGS** **MEANING** **EXAMPLE**	セン・ゼン・ぜに coin; .01 yen; money こぜに 小銭 small change; coins	金 metal; gold; money 二 two; 2 戈 spear, halberd He secretly hides the **gold** 金 *coin* and **two** 二 **halberds** 戈.

Do you have any questions? Anything confusing? Feel free to email me (Clay) at clay@thejapanshop.com with any questions, comments, or suggestions.

Do you have ideas to make *Makoto* better? We'd love to hear from you. Did something particularly help you? Love to hear that as well.

What to experience even more Makoto? Learn about our new Makoto+ membership. Download the latest issue or access web-based back issues. All this and more starting at only $3. Go to: **www.MakotoPlus.com** now!

Clay & Yumi